Pay It Forward

Home Business Funding Program

16 Years of Mail Order Success in a Step-By-Step Format That You Can Copy

AUDIO BOOK

24/7 RECORDING PLAYBACK: 804-242-0447
(55 minutes in length)

AUDIO AVAILABLE ONLINE: www.PIFaudiobook.com

COPYRIGHT NOTICE

PAY IT FORWARD
HOME BUSINESS FUNDING PROGRAM

© 2022 JOEL BROUGHTON ALL RIGHTS RESERVED

ISBN-13: 9798580316550

IF YOU INTEND TO COPY OR REPUBLISH ANY PART OF THIS BOOK, YOU MAY DO SO ONLY WITH PRIOR WRITTEN PERMISSION FROM THE AUTHOR AND COPYRIGHT HOLDER JOEL BROUGHTON.

Table of Contents

Introduction 5

Chapter 1: Start with the End Goal First 7

Chapter 2: The Easiest Way Doesn't Work 11

Chapter 3: Multiple Streams of Income Myth 18

Chapter 4: How Mail Order Works…Best 22

Chapter 5: One Straight Path To Success 27

Chapter 6: Why You Need High Ticket Sales 30

Chapter 7: Getting Set Up 1-2-3 33

AUDIO BOOK

24/7 RECORDING PLAYBACK: 804-242-0447
(55 minutes in length)

AUDIO AVAILABLE ONLINE:
www.PIFaudiobook.com

Joel Broughton

Introduction

My name is Joel Broughton and I want to welcome you to this new business venture that we are going to embark on together!

I have been self-employed, from home since 2004. As I write this book, it's been 16 years since I've held a job, answered to a boss, commuted to work, and received a paycheck from somebody else in exchange for my time.

I have earned a great living from the comfort of my home, using my laptop, my skills, and leveraging the power of direct mail marketing for the last 16 years…and I plan to continue for the next 16 years and beyond.

Throughout this book, you will get to know me personally, my successes and struggles in the Direct Mail Marketing industry. You'll learn how I originally ran multiple businesses – one in Direct Mail and one in Network Marketing and then focused on one to create the ultimate residual income machine. You will get to use this machine to make all your home-based business goals a reality.

Before I go on let me tell you this:

I am an expert in Direct Mail Marketing.

I am an expert in creating direct mail marketing systems

I am an expert in creating an income from home

…and I am willing to teach you what I know, so you can do it too!

Tony Robbins said it best:

"Most people have no idea of the giant capacity we can immediately command when we focus all of our resources on mastering a SINGLE AREA of our lives."

Chapter 1: Start with the End Goal First

A mentor of mine once asked me: "What is it that you are trying to accomplish with your business?" I replied simply "I want to get rich and live the life of my dreams."

He laughed. Not at me, but at what I said. "That's way too vague," he replied, "if you don't get specific about how much money you want to make and what exactly those dreams are…you will never accomplish anything."

After explaining to me the importance of goal setting, he left me with this immensely powerful quote from his friend the late Jim Rohn. I've kept this quote close to me throughout my home-based business career.

Jim said: **"I find it fascinating that most people plan their vacation with better care than they do their lives. Perhaps that is because escape is easier than change."**

Looking at this quote has always made me literally press pause on my LIFE BUTTON and take hours and sometimes even days to re-examine the path of life that I was heading down. Because what is more important than living my life to the fullest and fulfilling God's purpose for me and my family?

I know that living on autopilot doesn't get me any closer to any of my goals. Have you given up on your dreams and aspirations to work every day to help fulfill someone else's dreams? Are you working at a job you hate, with a boss you can't stand, for less pay than you deserve? It's not fun to wake up one day and realize that you spent a decade, or decades of your life working just to pay the bills and live an average life.

Joel Broughton

By the way, if you are content living an average life, in an average house, with an average car, working an average job, and getting paid the average in America…this book is not for you. You can stop reading now. What follows in this book is a blueprint to living an exceptional life, with an exceptional income, with exceptional time freedom!

Let me tell you a fast story.

In about 2005, I joined a network marketing company that offered an opportunity to sell a $10 product. My commissions on each new customer were $1 per member, per month. When I first joined this company, I thought this was a great commission. It paid out a 10% commission on each level (down 5 levels of members). This seemed like a good deal at the time.

We spent a couple of years piling in thousands of members into this company for the result of about $3,000 per month in commissions. Now you might be thinking, "Gee, $3,000 per month is a pretty good commission check…I'd be happy to make that from home." But that's not the point. The point is that if I had chosen to put those same 3000 people into a company that charged more and paid out more in commissions, then my check would be substantially higher.

The effort of selling an opportunity to 3,000 people is pretty much the same whether the opportunity costs them $10, $60, or $120. The commission however is significantly different. If I had set my goals on what total income I wanted to make, instead of deciding that the "deal" and commission % seemed good, I would have taken a different path.

In the same scenario, if the product we were selling cost $1200 and the commission rate was 10% or about $120 per member, then my overall commissions on 3,000 members would NOT have been a measly $3,000. My commissions would have been $360,000! It's incredible how a little bit of planning can change the trajectory of your income and your life.

That small realization was the same day that I vowed to never again earn a small $1 or $2 commission on anything that I sold. There had to be a large enough upside for me to make a decent monthly income.

Is it okay if we talk about you and your goals?

I've included a short exercise that I hope you will take seriously. Grab a pen and feel free to write your answers in this book. You'll be able to come back here months or years from now and see if you were able to accomplish exactly what you wanted. This will help you become more intentional and specific with your goal setting. When you complete this, you will be able to better identify what "business opportunities" can fit with what you are trying to accomplish. No more will you be falling for the next best thing that comes across your desk or into your mailbox.

Today's Date: _____

Question 1: What is your exact income goal?

_____

Question 2: Do you want to earn that money one-time or monthly?

_____

Question 3: What will you do with this money?

_____

I told you that it would be easy. I like to do things in bite sized chunks. That way you don't even feel like you're taking on the world. I don't ever want anything to hold you back on your journey to accomplishing YOUR goals.

As we dive deeper into how I've set up my business and success, you'll be able to copy (and even use my marketing systems) to fast-track your home-business and income goals. Have you ever heard the saying "It's not what you know, it's WHO you know"? I believe this is partially true. I believe that WHO you know 100% determines WHAT you know. Let me explain.

If you decide to wake up each day, go to work, talk to the same people, do the same tasks, and then go home and mindlessly watch sitcoms, news, or movies…your life will not change, your income will not change, and your dreams will stay far away.

By the way, I'm not judging you if you live your life this way. I'm just stating the obvious. If you don't change, your life won't change. Remember what Jim Rohn said: "Perhaps that is because <u>escape is easier than change</u>." If you let your mind be distracted, you'll remain in a small place for days, months, years and possibly even for a lifetime!

If you were guaranteed an income of $20,000 per month would you be willing to take one full day to read a book, talk to your team leader, and set up a business that could pay you that income for the rest of your life?

What if the income wasn't guaranteed, but just possible? Would you still be willing to sacrifice only one full day of your life to read a book, talk to your team leader, and set up a business that could pay you $20,000 per month for the rest of your life?

I don't know what your goals are. Maybe it's higher or lower than $20,000 per month. But my point is that you will need to start to prioritize what is important in your life, what sacrifices you are willing to make, and how important reaching your goal is to you.

If you decide to get to know me a little bit better, even partner with my team to build a successful home-based business, I want to be honest up front. There are going to be some sacrifices in time and money that you will need to make to start up and run a successful home-based business. This is the reality. Nothing in life is free...and nothing worth having comes easy.

My belief in business is that the ***"Easiest Way Doesn't Work"***. Business is not about doing something that's easy. That's what jobs are for. If you want something easy, get a job. You can show up for work, get told what to do and how to do it, collect a paycheck and go home and watch TV.

If you want to live the life of your dreams, you will have to commit to learning some new skills, talk to some new people (including your team leader), and change the path that you are currently on. Your family will thank you for it and you'll be proud of accomplishing something that most people only ever dream about. You'll be living the life of your dreams. Let's go get this together!

Chapter 2: The Easiest Way Doesn't Work

Let's start this chapter off with a BANG! If the easy way worked, everyone would already be rich.

There are thousands of so-called guru's, mentors, and program owners out there that are going to sell everyone what they want to buy – quick fix, quick money, overnight success. I'm not that guy. I'm not interested in selling you that and frankly if that's what you're looking for, then you can stop reading right now.

Success in a home-based business, I mean actual success, takes time to grow and develop. The great thing about it is that once you build up the skills, knowledge, and income through a home-based business, it can last a lifetime.

Joel Broughton

In 1999, I was ambushed after a nice dinner with a kitchen table presentation about a phenomenally successful network marketing business opportunity. I had never heard of network marketing before this and to be completely honest, after listening to the presentation and watching my future sponsor draw all the little houses on a page in the presentation booklet, I knew in my soul that this type of business was going to make me so rich!

After signing up they told me to make a "list of people I knew".

Thoughts were racing through my mind. I was starting to make a list of all the people I was going to immediately share it with. I couldn't believe that I was so privileged to be getting this information BEFORE anyone in my family or circle of friends had ever heard about it. I was the first. I was going to help them all quit their jobs and become rich like me. They would all be so excited to hear about this opportunity.

When I got home, my mind was racing with excitement. I couldn't believe my family had never heard about this type of business before. If they had, they'd all be in it and would have told me about it, right? Like I said, they were all going to join so that they could shop from our own store and make money from home.

I followed the advice of my sponsor who told me to wait until he was going to be back in my city, and he would come do the presentations for me. This was great because I knew that he would explain the business a lot better than I ever could. He also told me that when I booked the appointments, I should not tell my prospects (family and friends) anything about the business.

I couldn't even tell them the name of the company because he said it was a "visual thing" and they would have to see it to really understand. I wasn't allowed to explain any of it over the phone and he emphasized "No telling anyone the company name". I thought it was a little bit bizarre to not tell them the company name, but I felt like he must have known what he was doing.

I booked my first appointment with my uncle. I did exactly what I was supposed to. I called him on the phone, told him that I had a business to show him, but that I couldn't go through anything on the phone. I asked if my business partner and I could stop by to go over some details with him.

He agreed and we were set. I was extremely nervous, but I think it was just the excitement of the possibility that my uncle would be joining the business. He was older than me (of course) and knew a lot of people. Together we were going to get so many more business partners and customers. This was going to be great.

So, my sponsor picked me up in his rental car and we drove out to my uncle's house. My sponsor wore a nice suit, white shirt, red tie. He said that dressing up was important when I started to do the presentations myself and that I should always wear a red tie.

As we walked up the front steps, he told me to let him do all the talking and make sure I paid close attention to the presentation because very soon I would be able to do the presentations for my growing team. I was ecstatic.

My uncle let us in and walked us to the living room. My sponsor asked if we could sit at the kitchen table instead, but my uncle insisted on the living room since they had stuff piled on the kitchen table. They talked back and forth for a minute as my sponsor insisted, he needed that table. They finally agreed on the dining room. (I guess there was something special about having to do the presentation at the kitchen table).

As we sat down at the dining room table and as my sponsor reached for his presentation booklet from his case on the floor my uncle suddenly said, "This isn't Amway is it? Because if this is Amway, I don't want anything to do with it."

Joel Broughton

> *(As a side note Amway is a large successful network marketing company but over the years has got a negative reputation among some people.)*

My sponsor responded and tried to find out what my uncle knew about the company and why he was feeling like he didn't want to see the presentation now. I couldn't believe what I was hearing.

My mind was screaming "SHOW HIM THE HOUSES!!! SHOW HIM HOW WE ALL GET RICH WITH THIS!!!" but I said nothing.

I just sat there in disbelief as my uncle told us to "Get out!" There was no way that he wanted anything to do with us. There was no way he would even let me "practice" by showing him the business presentation. He literally wanted nothing to do with it.

As we were quickly ushered out of his home, I experienced a great feeling of rejection and humiliation. But the most intense feeling I had at that moment was of confusion. What had just happened? How did that happen? I didn't get it.

Over the next few weeks, I learned that my own Mom also didn't want to see the presentation. She wouldn't even agree to an appointment unless I told her the company name and when I did that, she also refused to even look at it with me and my sponsor.

My Amway business was short lived. I recruited exactly ZERO people. I did have one friend that desperately wanted to join with me, but I avoided his calls for weeks and eventually we lost touch. I didn't want to sign him up in this business that might cause him so much rejection and humiliation. I didn't talk to him again…ever.

I jumped at the chance to build my business the easy way. Talk to friends and family, they'll love this, then they'll talk to their friends and everyone will join and get rich. Unfortunately, that method does not work.

Pay It Forward Home Business Funding Program

Disclaimer: I will share my direct mail marketing business with friends and family IF they ask about it and want to start their own home-based business. But I do not chase them all in hopes that they'll build a huge business for me.

I now understand that a real business requires advertising. Actual advertising to find real members and customers. I'm guessing that you already understand this concept that you will need to advertise if you want to grow a successful home-based business. When I first started, I didn't know this, but I know it better than most now.

The next thing I learned, I got lucky with this, was that it's better to sell "how to" build a home-based business prior to selling the business opportunity itself. I literally fell into this concept by accident.

I was travelling with the military, sitting on an airplane, and I remember it like it was yesterday. Flipping through a big city newspaper (yes, newspapers were still a thing back then), I came across an ad in the business opportunity section of the classifieds. It read something like this: "Make $1500 per week, PT, call for details".

Just my luck! I had stumbled into another PERFECT opportunity. I was a little more cautious this time I called for details and waited for the information to arrive at my home. A small info pack letter was mailed to me and I immediately loved what I read. This was my first experience in the Direct Mail industry. I sent in for my money-making package and distributor kit that the letter offered, and I was on my way to riches!

Within about a week, I received my distributor kit and fast start instructions. It said to call the number for a Business Coach. My business coach then proceeded to sell me $4,000 worth of promotional materials, products, flyers, and business cards that I would need for my new business. I was on my way.

One day I'll tell you the whole story about this failure. For brevity sake today, I'll say that the business model they had set up for me to use and promote was not all it was built up to be. I think I made sales of about $200 (and that's probably being generous). My total loss for that opportunity would be in the range of $4,000 - $6,000 when I finally decided to move on.

I always like to focus on the bright side of business failure. I learn something, meet someone, or at least learn what not to do.

In this business, I joined one of the owners of this company in a new network marketing business. He had joined and was running his direct mail company and building a network marketing company on the side. We became friends and I spent hours on the phone listening to him masterfully sell the network marketing business to prospects.

He forced me to face my fears of rejection, learn how to sell on the phone, and understand how to close sales in a way that made everyone happy to join or buy. He gave me sales training CD's to listen to while we worked together. Tom Hopkins was one of the sales trainers that he shared with me and I remember Tom saying this one simple statement: **"I am not judged by the number of times I fail, but by the number of times I succeed; and the number of times I succeed is in direct proportion to the number of times I can fail and keep on trying."**

I will always get up and try again, no matter how many times I fail. Derek, if you ever read this book one day "I am forever grateful for the time and patience you had for me as I began a successful journey to the top of the network marketing industry. You will always be a cherished friend!"

Derek was the best salesman I had ever met, but it was his business partner that knew the advertising, mail order and lead generation side of the business and that's the next thing that took my income to a whole new level. When I got to look on the inside of a mail order operation and what it really took to make it, I was sold on this being _the best business model in the world_. I modelled exactly what they were doing and over the years have made it better and faster for all my members, friends, and business partners to use.

I now had the keys to the castle. I now understood what it really took to build a successful home-based business. It wasn't the easy way of chasing around friends and family. It wasn't the easy way of promoting my business directly to people hoping they would jump on board.

Building my business using direct mail worked.

1. True, building a business using a direct mail system is slower than just pitching everyone you know.

2. True, sending letters or postcards through the mail to prospects is slower than running ads on Facebook. True, fulfilling orders for books, programs, and courses is slower than bringing people to an online webinar.

3. But it's also true that using a direct mail system to generate long-term residual income in a direct mail marketing business works better than anything that other people are doing today.

So, let me ask you a few questions.

Today's Date: _____

Question 1: Can you be patient and stick with the same business for over 12 months?

_____

Question 2: Are you willing to start learning some new skills?

_____

Question 3: Are you willing to spend money advertising your business?

I don't look at how easy something is. I look at how EFFECTIVE it is. Does it work? Can it work for all my team? Can it work for you too?

The answer with a direct mail marketing system is:

Yes, Yes, and YES!

Chapter 3: Multiple Streams of Income Myth

I was sold a lie. Maybe you bought this lie too. It's called "Multiple Streams of Income", the best way to build wealth.

It took me years and many failures to realize that multiple streams of income are not for beginners or people starting out. Let me explain.

A few years into my home-based business career I started "collecting" businesses. Anytime I saw a new business opportunity through the mail or online that looked good I joined it immediately. Have you ever done this? If so, then you probably know what a waste of money this was for me.

All these businesses I joined seemed so great at the time, but there was one problem. And it wasn't the businesses I was joining. Time was my problem. I couldn't possibly promote and build all these businesses at the same time. Trying to build one successful mail order business or downline in a network marketing company is hard enough, much less trying to build 2, or 3, or 5…like I was doing.

I look back today and think of how ridiculous it was to try to build more than one main income stream in network marketing or direct mail. But I was sold the dream of multiple streams of income and I believed in it.

Before I explain to you why the idea of multiple streams of income is NOT a good idea when you are trying to build your business, let me tell you a quick story.

Over several years I built up a successful direct mail company that sold various products and opportunities through the mail. It was a straight mail order operation. Prospects would answer an ad, we'd mail them a letter, they'd mail back a check, money order or credit card and we'd mail them their product. The sale ended there.

I was frustrated with the process because every time I sold a product, I had to start over with running an ad again. There was no recurring sales and no residual income. I kept asking myself how I could generate so many new customers last month and then must start over again this month with more new customers and new sales. It felt like a never-ending cycle of work.

I decided that the solution was network marketing. I was already doing both anyway, so I decided to spend more time building my network marketing business and less time on the mail order side. My network marketing business flourished. I won trips, bonuses, big commissions…and my mail order business dwindled.

Oops. All the time I was spending building my network marketing business took away from my mail order business. So, I started focusing on my mail order business again and my network marketing business started to suffer. But don't worry I knew exactly what to do.

I set up an online marketing system for my network marketing team and sold memberships to the website and training. Once again, my network marketing business grew, the online marketing system grew, and my mail order business suffered. How is this possible? All the money gurus told me to have multiple streams of income. What was I doing wrong?

Let me explain what I now know. Multiple streams of income only include 1 active stream of income. There are two types of income "active" and "passive". Active means that you are spending time building that income. This can be through a job, a home-based business, an online business or running your own company. These are all active because you must spend your time to make the money.

Passive income means money that you are getting to spend no time doing it. Stocks can be passive if you invest and hold. Real Estate can be passive if you buy and hold…but don't spend time building your portfolio. Social Security checks are passive. Investments can be passive. Network marketing and direct mail are NOT passive.

For me, the terms were very confusing early on because I would think that passive income was the same as residual income. Residual income is of course money that comes in monthly (but you do normally still have to work for it).

> Multiple Streams of Income = more than one paycheck
> Passive Income = money with zero time invested
> Active income = money with time invested
> Residual Income = money that comes in monthly

All this to just say that I thought building up multiple businesses would give me multiple streams of income. Instead, it just gave me less income and more problems. I was also chasing a new business, new opportunity, or better way of making money, instead of just sticking with what was working well.

Today, I now run my business with my mail order (and a multi-level component of it) combined into one simple system that allows for them to work harmoniously. The mail order business has multiple levels of payments in it, so I don't need a network marketing business or product (and you won't either).

Pay It Forward Home Business Funding Program

Before we wrap this up let me ask you if you know how these people make their money:

1. Sam Walton
2. Bill Gates
3. Jeff Bezos
4. Donald Trump
5. Steve Jobs
6, Walt Disney

None of them made their wealth through "multiple streams of income". They might have multiple streams now through investments in different stocks, companies, or industries. But they all made their money by becoming an expert in one industry and with one company.

(Sam Walton – Walmart, Bill Gates – Microsoft, Jeff Bezos – Amazon, Donald Trump – Real Estate, Steve Jobs – iPhone, Walt Disney – Entertainment)

Sam Walton didn't build Walmart and at the same time try to revolutionize the real estate world. Jeff Bezos didn't build Amazon into online selling behemoth and at the same time build family friendly theme parks. None of these success stories actively built more than one company or in one industry at a time.

That's the model that I am going to follow. Actively build one company in one industry. Answer the questions below and make a commitment that will change your life.

Today's Date: _____

Question 1: Can you **actively build** more than one direct mail or network marketing company at the same time?

_____

Question 2: Are you willing to quit all other home-based business, opportunities, direct mail programs, and network marketing businesses if I can show you how to succeed in one?

_____

Question 3: Are you willing to follow me (and my team), a top leader in direct mail marketing?

If you answered Yes to Questions 2 and 3 above, then here is my challenge to you. In the next 3-5 days, quit, throw out, cancel ALL other home-based business, direct mail programs or network marketing businesses that you currently are in or spend money in.

This isn't going to be easy for you. You've probably spent time, money, and energy in these other businesses…but if you really want to succeed in a big way, I need you to make the commitment to yourself and our new business venture together.

The famous inventor Alexander Graham Bell said: **"When one door closes another door opens; but we often look so long and so regretfully upon the closed door that we do not see the one which has opened for us."**

Most of us have only heard the first part of that quote. The important part is the latter. If we focus too much on the past, we can't welcome a bright future with open arms or even recognize it when it comes. If you are stuck in so many "opportunities" and businesses and making barely any money or no money in them, I'm here today to tell you that <u>it's okay to let them all go!</u>

Chapter 4: How Mail Order Works…Best

In 2004, I had written my first business booklet as a promotional tool to build my business. I taught my customers how to make money by using a simple direct mail process. The booklet was only about 20 pages long, but it described how they could use the same marketing system that I was using to build a successful Direct Mail Marketing business.

Here's how it worked. I ran a simple classified advertisement in the Business Opportunities section of daily and weekly newspapers. Through the ad, I directed my prospects to a simple one-page website which explain the business. I explained to them that my marketing system would help them succeed in a home-based business and for only $12.95, I would send them my business booklet.

Once they received the booklet, they would be directed to call me to discuss getting fully set up in the business. I would then call them (or have one of my team members call) and invite them to an overview of our opportunity on one of our daily calls. After hearing our presentation call, they could join the direct mail marketing company and participate in a co-operative advertising program to help generate leads for their business.

I continued to run more advertising, sell more booklets, invite to presentations, close the sales, and repeat the process with all the new team members. This allowed everyone to participate in getting sales and succeeding in the opportunity. By using this marketing system, I created, several people began earning a full-time income, and many others were earning a significant part-time income from home.

The success of this marketing system was attributed to three specific things.

1. The marketing system identified "buyers" by selling them the $12.95 booklet before we spoke to them about our direct mail marketing opportunity. This step in my process pre-qualified the good prospects without spending any of our time to do it.

2. The marketing system generated up front money through the sales of the booklets. This money was then re-invested to run more advertising to generate more sales. Re-investing is necessary for growth.

3. The marketing system offered the prospects specifically what they were looking for. It first sold them a PLAN on "How To Make Money From Home", instead of selling them the actual business opportunity. (We gave them the solution – how to do it, instead of just giving them another problem – a new business). The booklet was designed to do this because the prospects were specifically trying to figure out how to make money, they weren't necessarily trying to buy into a direct mail marketing company.

Try to remember when you are talking to your prospects and your team that they deep down just want to know **WHAT TO DO** and **HOW TO DO IT**.

Did you know that most of the time, prospects are not looking to buy your products or services? They are looking for you to show them how to solve their problems…and specifically in this industry "HOW" to make money from home.

You see, this marketing system worked so well because I offered the "how to succeed" prior to offering the actual opportunity. I offered a solution first. By the time the prospects got to the actual business, they already understood what they were going to do to make money. They already fully understood how they were going to have success. So, the moment that they saw the network marketing opportunity, they understood that this was simply the vehicle that they would use to get paid. The marketing system and advertising program was what was going to generate the results and income.

In my business, I have perfected the ability to show people "what to do" and "how to do it". I perfected the ability to get people to purchase the marketing system before knowing all the details about the business.

In fact, as proof, you are a great example. You purchased this marketing system without knowing all the details about the business. You are reading now about "what to do" and "how to do it" – simply mail letters like I did to generate sales and prospects.

The reason why my prospects don't mind joining my business without knowing everything is because I gain their trust throughout the process. I show them that their success is dependent on the process, not just on a product. It's dependent on the advertising and marketing, not on a compensation plan. And by the time they get to see the great products that I am offering, they tell me they would have joined regardless of what product I was selling…BUT they are so happy that I picked something to offer.

I believe that your customers will buy anything you have to sell:

> **IF** you gain their trust
> **IF** you always deliver quality
> **IF** you do what you say you're going to do
> **IF** you are honest
> **IF** you make them as important as yourself

Your customers will be able to feel if they can trust you or not. I'd rather be honest with someone and have them walk away from the business, then lie to them just to make a sale. Businesspeople that lie to their customers end up being someone else's employees because you can't build a business without trust.

Even to this day when I work on my marketing system or training, I always try to think: "Will this help my team?" If the answer is YES, I continue. If the answer is NO, then I stop and work on something that will help them. I believe that my success is solely based on leverage and the cumulative success of my team.

Leverage only comes when my team is willing to work with me. And my team is only willing to work with me if I truly show them all how to make the income they desire. This is how I have built huge teams. This is how I continue to build huge teams, and this is how you too can build your own huge team.

My offers are always amazingly simple. I always sell the "How To" first. Then I follow with the actual opportunity. In fact, right now today, you are a prime example of the way I sell. You joined my marketing system first on how to make money from home. Your first exposure wasn't to the place where I make all the big money in this industry – my direct mail marketing opportunity. Your first exposure was to the purchase of this book and marketing system.

So, let me ask you this:

Today's Date: _____

Question 1: Do your customers want the product that you're selling OR do they want a solution to their problem?

_____

Question 2: Are you willing to be honest with your customers and team?

_____

Question 3: What are you going to sell to your customers? Will you sell them "How To" solve their problem or will you sell them yet another problem?

_____

Although I'd been using these methods for years before coming across an online training by Perry Marshall, I absolutely love what he says and thus I want to share it with you: **"Nobody who bought a drill actually wanted a drill. They wanted a hole. Therefore, if you want to sell drills you should advertise information about making holes – NOT information about drills."**

Chapter 5: One Straight Path To Success

When I finally added a multi-level part of my direct mail business that's when my life and my business started to get fun (and profitable) for me and my team. For years, I had run my direct mail business myself and not allowing others to profit as well. Then one day I had the realization that we could all make even more money together if I taught everyone how to do it and set up the actual system for them to use as well.

I made the decision to make it easy on myself and my team. Direct mail is the lead generation side of the business. The upsells and the High Ticket sale is the money-making side of the business. By streamlining everything, I'm now able to run one big successful team that uses my expertly built direct mail systems to drive prospects through the system and into our High Ticket business.

Success in your business and your life is about making the right decisions at the right times and going down the correct path that will lead you to the fulfillment of your goals and dreams.

One of my favorite speakers in our industry, Zig Ziglar once said: **"Lack of direction, not lack of time, is the problem. We all have twenty-four-hour days."**

A few people choose not to join our High Ticket business, and simply use the systems and the upgrades/upsells to make money…but to be honest they are kind of missing out on the best part of my marketing systems, which is the bigger income.

The Pay It Forward Home Business Funding Program works the same way all my direct mail marketing systems work. Below is the exact system you can use to make good money from home. If you follow the instructions, stay consistent and work with me, you too can be one of our next big success stories!

The Pay It Forward Home Business Funding Program works like this:

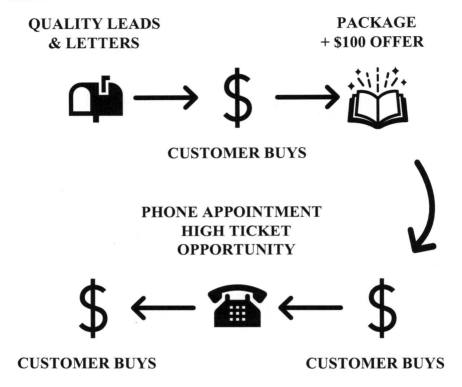

You can get paid 3 times for doing 1 mailing!

You can do the mailings yourself or we'll do them for you. Then your customer will send you a payment along with 2 other payments, one that comes to our monitor and one that goes to your direct sponsor. Next, we'll send your customer this exact book and the option to upgrade to the higher level in the Pay It Forward Home Business Funding Program for 3 payments of $100…one of those payments will be mailed directly to YOU!

Then finally, we book phone appointments with all your customers for you (you don't have to do any sales or selling). We talk to your customers and if they decide to participate in the high ticket opportunity, then they are placed direct to you in your and you get paid AGAIN! That's 3 checks (or cash) for doing one simple advertising activity by mailing the original letter.

Remember, all you do is just join the business with us, then mail the letters and we take care of the rest. We mail the packages, we do all the phone sales, we sign up your customers for you in the high ticket opportunity. It's all turnkey and simple for you and all your members.

When your new team mails the letters and starts to get their own customers, you can get paid on those too. Because you are the new upline for this member you will get $20 and $100 payments on all their new customers and this money is sent directly to you. Then when their new customers also join the high ticket opportunity, they'll also be in your team and you can get paid again, this time a big payment!

Let's make a commitment to start building a successful business together:

Today's Date: _____

Question 1: Will you commit to starting your advertising immediately so you can start making money?

_____

Question 2: Will you commit to upgrading to the additional 2 STEPS of the marketing system if it fits within your budget?

_____

Question 3: What part of this marketing system so far has you the most excited?

_____

It's such a nice surprise for you to see that you do advertising once, you can get paid up to 3 times, and get a huge payment from all your new customers.

Chapter 6: Why You Need The High Ticket Opportunity

The High Ticket part of this program is the cornerstone of the income opportunity. It's the place that you can build your long-term income. It's the place where people are getting life-changing income and falling in love with the business.

The mail order and upgrade pieces are essential to making this all work. But the High Ticket business is where the real money is being made.

SPECIAL NOTE: *If the High Ticket opportunity fits within your budget to join, please contact us to join immediately so we can start to build your commissions with it. If it doesn't fit within your budget today, don't worry, you can get started as soon as you possibly can.*

In the meantime, let's start advertising the Pay It Forward program and start generating some leads and cashflow for you so that you can make enough to join the High Ticket business and grow your income. The sooner you can join us, the better!

By now you might be asking why is this program is called the "Pay It Forward Home Business Funding Program"? It's quite simple.

The Pay It Forward name originated back in 2005 from an online marketing system I started and built to over 240,000 members. It's a throw-back to that system, but it also has special meaning to me.

Pay It Forward Home Business Funding Program

I'm "Paying It Forward" to you by teaching you everything I've learned about marketing, advertising and direct mail marketing. By teaching you and allowing you to use my marketing systems I'm "Paying It Forward" to you in thanks to all the great mentors and teachers I've had throughout the years.

I want you to build a huge team using this same system and by sharing this with others through your advertising, you will be "Paying It Forward" to these new people too. People that are struggling just to make ends meet, living on social security, miserable in their job, or just outright need more money to live their dream life! You don't know it today, but by you joining us and promoting the Pay It Forward program, you could be impacting 100's or even 1000's of lives for the better. Somewhere in the United States, right now, someone is praying for the opportunity to change their income and their life, and you can be the one to share it with them!

The "Home Business Funding Program" relates directly to the marketing system. The marketing system generates money for you through the sales of the marketing system and this Home Business Funding Program book. It also generates money for you on autopilot through the upgrade process that's included with your package.

All this initial money that's generated is what you can use to advertise your business, upgrade your business, and pay for all the expenses in your business. That's what I call "Home Business Funding". The business provides the funding to continually run new advertising to grow your business bigger, virtually on autopilot, for you.

Those 2 simple payments that are made to you by your customers can create a regular stream of income for you that may cover all your advertising and mailing expenses. And if all your expenses are paid for through the marketing system…then all the income that you get through the High Ticket opportunity is then pure profit!

The importance of the High Ticket business is to provide the profitability of the business. This is where you make the money to pay your bills, quit your job, go on vacations, buy new cars, and live the life of your dreams.

If you don't believe me, ask the best-selling author of Rich Dad, Poor Dad, Mr. Robert Kiyosaki. In an interview he said: **"If I had to do it all over again, rather than build an old-style type of business, I would have started building a home based marketing business."**

My initial instinct about making money from home when I first saw it back in 1999 was absolutely, 100% correct. <u>I can get rich in the home based business industry</u>. So, can you! But the methods and systems that we use to build our team are significantly different than the ones I was taught back then.

The High Ticket opportunity provides the big income opportunity that you need to really have success. When any of your members promote and get new members into their team…you get paid. You get paid even though all you did was find the first member in the team. Then we call and do all the selling for you. You never will be asked to get on the phone to sell or close prospects, this is all taken care of automatically by your Team Leader.

Pretty cool, right?

The High Ticket opportunity also does MOST of the work for you. Here's a short list of things we are happy to do:

1. We are going to accept all the payments
2. We are going to ship the products
3. We are going to track the commissions
4. We are going to pay you your commissions
5. We are going to do the customer service
6. We are going to do all the accounting

All you need to do is refer members through the simple Pay It Forward program. To refer members, you'll mail the initial letters selling the program. I'll then fulfill the packages for you, process the upgrades, and do all the phone appointments and enrolments into the High Ticket business.

Knowing what you know now about how the entire system works, let re-visit your goals and write them down:

Today's Date: _____

Question 1: What is your exact income goal?

_____

Question 2: Do you want to earn that money one-time or monthly?

_____

Question 3: Will you commit to a 12-24-month plan to achieve the goals above?

_____

Chapter 7: Getting Set Up 1-2-3

I'm so glad that you've made it this far. To be fair, there are some people that purchase this program and don't even read it through. Then they wonder why they're not making any money yet. You are special and you are going to succeed with our business.

If you're considering getting started but are not sure of exactly how everything will play out, it's okay. You don't need to know how everything works, just that it does work! Martin Luther King Jr once said: **"Take the first step in faith. You don't have to see the whole staircase, just take the first step."**

Joel Broughton

Let's cut right to the chase on what it takes to get started on the path to making the income that you want from this business.

I am here to support you and help you. I don't give out my personal cell phone and email address to everyone that receives this book, but once you join our High Ticket opportunity, I'll be happy to speak with you, text with you or email with you to support you in your success in building a large business with an income to match!

To our success together!

Joel Broughton
Founder Pay It Forward Home Business Funding Program

Pay It Forward Home Business Funding Program

FIRST: Upgrade STEP 2 of your Pay It Forward business. Complete the upgrade form that we included in your package. Mail the payments to the 3 people listed on the form. Once those are received you will be totally set up to maximize your income with the Pay It Forward system.

Although the upgrade is optional – you can do this business without upgrading. I would highly recommend that you take that step to maximize every dollar of income that is due to you through your advertising efforts.

SECOND: Get set up in the STEP 3: High Ticket opportunity. Contact your Team Leader now to get more details on the High Ticket opportunity and to get set up. You can book an appointment online, or call or text your team leader today.

Your team leader will handle all the calls, sales, training, and managing this part of the business for you and your entire team. This is the easiest way to build an income ever created!

THIRD: Start doing some mailings. This is the lifeblood of your business. The best way to grow your business is to set up a regular consistent advertising plan for yourself. You can set up an automatic monthly payment for the letters to be mailed out for you or have them shipped to your home for you to apply postage and mail them yourself.

Either way you choose will be fine, the importance is in being consistent. Weekly or monthly mailings will get you to your goals the fastest. If you don't stay consistent, it will take longer to reach your income goals.

Joel Broughton

Pay It Forward Home Business Funding Program

Joel Broughton

Pay It Forward Home Business Funding Program

EARNINGS DISCLAIMER

PAY IT FORWARD: THE HOME BUSINESS FUNDING PROGRAM IS A BOOK THAT DISCUSSES MY BUSINESS PAY IT FORWARD HOME BUSINESS FUNDING PROGRAM, WHICH IS A MARKETING COMPANY THAT SELLS LETTERS, POSTCARDS, LEADS, ONLINE MARKETING TRAINING SYSTEMS AND INFORMATION PRODUCTS. OUR PAY IT FORWARD HOME BUSINESS FUNDING PROGRAM CUSTOMERS ALSO HAVE THE OPTION OF BECOMING AFFILIATE MEMBERS WHERE THEY CAN EARN COMMISSIONS BY REFERRING CUSTOMERS TO OUR PRODUCTS AND SERVICES. MANY OF OUR MEMBERS ALSO EARN INCOME BY SELLING OTHER COMPANY'S PRODUCTS TO CUSTOMERS THAT THEY ATTRACTED USING OUR MARKETING LETTERS, POSTCARDS AND ONLINE SYSTEMS.

ALL EARNINGS OR INCOME STATEMENTS BY OUR COMPANY AND ANY OF OUR AFFILIATE MEMBERS ON OUR WEBSITES, SALES LETTERS, BOOKS, POSTCARDS, OR ANY OTHER MATERIAL NOT OWNED BY US BUT REFERRING TO OUR BUSINESS ARE ONLY ESTIMATES OR EXAMPLES OF WHAT IS POSSIBLE AND WHAT SOME PEOPLE HAVE EARNED. THERE IS NO ASSURANCE OR GUARANTEE THAT YOU'LL EARN A SIMILAR INCOME, OR THAT YOU WILL EARN ANY INCOME AT ALL. EARNINGS AND INCOME EARNED WITH OUR COMPANY OR USING OUR PRODUCTS AND SERVICES ARE STILL 100% BASED ON YOUR EFFORTS TO BUILD YOUR OWN INDEPENDENT BUSINESS SUCCESS. WE DO NOT TAKE ANY RESPONSIBILITY FOR YOUR SUCCESS OR FAILURE BY USING ANY OF OUR PRODUCTS, SERVICES, WEBSITES, OR MARKETING SYSTEMS.

ANY AND ALL CLAIMS, REPRESENTATIONS, TESTIMONIALS OR INCOME OR RESULTS USING OUR PRODUCTS, SERVICES, WEBSITES, OR MARKETING SYSTEMS ARE NOT TO BE CONSIDERED AS AVERAGE RESULTS. OUR TESTIMONIALS COME FROM A WIDE RANGE OF MEMBERS FROM BEGINNERS TO TOP EARNERS AND WE CANNOT GUARANTEE YOU WILL GET SIMILAR RESULTS BY FOLLOWING THE SAME BUSINESS MODEL THEY ARE USING.

WE REPRESENT THE POTENTIAL OF OUR BUSINESS TO THE BEST OF OUR ABILITY BASED ON OUR SUCCESS USING THE METHODOLOGIES THAT WE TEACH AND THE MARKETING MATERIALS THAT WE SELL. HOWEVER, THERE CAN BE NO ASSURANCE THAT ANY PRIOR SUCCESS, PAST RESULTS, OR SUCCESS OF OTHER PEOPLE WILL TRANSLATE TO INCOME OR SUCCESS FOR YOU. THERE IS NO ASSURANCE THAT ANY PAST SUCCESS CAN BE USED TO INDICATE ANY FUTURE INCOME OR RESULTS WITH OUR BUSINESS.

YOUR INCOME RESULTS ARE FIRST AND FOREMOST BASED ON YOU. WE HAVE NO WAY TO PREDICT YOUR RESULTS WITH OUR BUSINESS SINCE WE DO NOT KNOW YOU, YOUR BACKGROUND, YOUR BUSINESS ACUMEN, SKILLS, WORK ETHIC, CONTACTS, OR ANY OTHER FACTOR THAT CONTRIBUTES TO SUCCESS IN YOUR OWN PERSONAL BUSINESS. WE DO NOT GUARANTEE OR IMPLY THAT YOU WILL GET RICH, BE ABLE TO QUIT YOUR JOB, OR MAKE ANY MONEY AT

Joel Broughton

ALL. THERE IS NO GUARANTEE THAT YOU WILL GET THE SAME RESULTS OF OTHER PEOPLE USING THE SAME BUSINESS MODEL AND MARKETING MATERIALS.

HOME BASED BUSINESSES, MAIL ORDER BUSINESSES, AND ONLINE BUSINESSES HAVE UNKNOWN RISKS AND ARE NOT SUITABLE FOR EVERYONE. YOU SHOULD MAKE YOUR OWN PERSONAL DECISION IF THIS BUSINESS IS RIGHT FOR YOU BEFORE STARTING OR JOINING THIS OR ANY BUSINESS ONLINE. YOU ARE FULLY RESPONSIBLE FOR YOUR OWN DECISION TO JOIN AND PROMOTE THIS OR ANY RELATED BUSINESS AND WE DO NOT ACCEPT ANY RESPONSIBILITY FOR YOUR SUCCESS OR FAILURE BY ENGAGING OUR COMPANY'S PRODUCTS AND SERVICES.

Made in the USA
Middletown, DE
13 November 2022

14581984R00024